The Torrie Collection · Talbot Rice Gallery
University of Edinburgh

Jacob Isaacksz van Ruisdael *The Banks of a River*, 1649 (see page 39)

DUNCAN MACMILLAN

A CATALOGUE OF THE
TORRIE
COLLECTION

THE UNIVERSITY · OF EDINBURGH

Published in the UK in 2004 by
Talbot Rice Gallery · The University of Edinburgh
Old College · South Bridge
Edinburgh EH8 9YL

For further information contact the
Talbot Rice Gallery, telephone 0131 650 2210
or visit our website: www.trg.ed.ac.uk

ISBN 1 873 108 45 1

Designed and typeset in Manticore by Dalrymple
Printed by BAS Printers Ltd, Salisbury

Front cover: Adam Pynacker *A Forest Glade*

Back cover: Francois Duquesnoy
(il Flamingo) *Cupid*

THE PUBLICATION OF THIS CATALOGUE
HAS BEEN SUPPORTED BY

Charles Stanley
STOCKBROKERS

Talbot Rice Gallery

Sir Thomas Lawrence *Portrait of Sir James Erskine of Torrie Bt*
Courtesy of the Trustees of the Dunimarle Trust

FOREWORD

The first catalogue of the Torrie Collection was published in 1837 on behalf of the trustees of Sir James Erskine of Torrie's will. Its publication marked the final transfer of his collection to the University under the terms of the will. A few years later the collection was loaned to the Royal Institution and passed from it to its successor body, the new National Gallery of Scotland. From that time forward the Torrie Collection was catalogued as part of the national collection, though the University continued to include a list of the works in the collection in its annual calendar. The bulk of the collection was returned to the University in 1954, but the catalogue research undertaken in the National Gallery over the years formed the basis of the catalogue published in 1983. Important contributions to cataloguing the sculpture were also made by Anthony Radcliffe and Charles Avery, however, and also later by Elizabeth Wilson. The 1983 catalogue marked the final return to the University of the small group of works that at that date still remained on loan to the National

Gallery though since then the great painting by Ruisdael, *The Banks of a River*, and a number of small sculptures have gone back on loan the National Gallery. The present catalogue updates the 1983 publication. It includes new research where possible, though many of the entries remain summary, and also for the first time illustrates much of the collection.

Publication of this new catalogue has been made possible by the generosity of John Torrie, Ian Harley and Christopher Clayhills-Henderson of Charles Stanley Stockbrokers who generously continued the support for the project initiated by Torrie & Co when they acquired that company. The Friends of the Talbot Rice Gallery have also made a generous contribution. To these benefactors and to all those who have assisted in the preparation of this catalogue, both now and in the past, I extend my grateful thanks.

DUNCAN MACMILLAN, *Curator*

The Edinburgh University Museum, *c.*1830
Designed by Willam Henry Playfair, the former University Museum
is now home to The Torrie Collection

INTRODUCTION

Sir James Erskine, third Baronet of Torrie, was an art collector of note, but professionally he was a very successful soldier. He was born in 1772 at Torrie House in Fife and began his military career in 1788, rising to Lieutenant Colonel in 1794 and full Colonel in 1800. Between 1802 and 1804 he was ADC to King George III, but in spite of the tensions between the king and his eldest son, he was also a friend of the Prince Regent, himself a major collector, particularly of Dutch art. Sir James served with Wellington and was with him in Paris after the fall of Napoleon. He ended his career with the rank of Lieutenant General. Wellington himself also formed a fine collection, so Sir James's taste for art as a soldier was not unprecedented.

When exactly he began to collect and the circumstances in which he developed his collection are unclear however. Certainly he was not just following fashion, for he was himself an amateur artist of some talent and the full extent of his collection, now divided between the University of Edinburgh and the National Gallery of Scotland's outpost at Duff House, on loan from the Dunimarle Trust, indicates a real passion for art. His own surviving work suggests that as an artist he was very close to David Allan. This is explained by the fact that Allan, whose father was harbour master in Alloa, was himself a protégée of the Erskines along with other local families connected to them and he no doubt acted as art teacher to these families in return for their support. James, who was the second son and inherited the title on the death of his brother William in 1813, appears as a boy along with his parents and his six siblings in a family portrait by Allan posed outside Torrie House and now preserved at Dunimarle, the house that his sister, Margaret Sharpe Erskine later built. Significantly,

too, from 1786 till his death ten years later, Allan was himself Master of the Trustees Academy and the Academy was housed in the University, by his will of 1824 the eventual destination for the bulk of Sir James's collection, or the Torrie collection as it became known.

There is some evidence that Sir James may have begun collecting quite early in the nineteenth century. He was certainly still buying art shortly before his death in 1825, so the collection was formed during those first two decades of the century. The emphasis is on the art of the seventeenth century and to an extent that reflects the taste of the time as it is seen in contemporary collections like that of the Prince Regent, or the Bourgeois Collection formed in the 1790s and bequeathed to Dulwich College in 1811. The Scottish painter-dealer Andrew Wilson certainly contributed to the formation of the collection, but by his own account Wilson himself had no taste for Dutch painting until he was introduced to it by Wilkie around 1811 which suggests that the bulk of the collection may have been formed after that date. Collecting certainly seems more likely to have been a peacetime than a wartime activity for a soldier on active service in a period of constant war. There are doubtless exceptions to that however. The marble *Venus* by Ponçet, for instance, is very likely to have been acquired when Sir James was in Paris during the occupation of the city by the Duke of Wellington and his troops in 1815. Perhaps other works, such as the painting by Greuze, *Interior of a Cottage*, have a similar origin. Until we have more information about the provenance of his pictures however, this must remain speculation. Sir James had a house in London and the bulk of the collection is certainly most likely to have been acquired on the art market there.

Numerically Dutch painting forms the bulk of the Torrie collection and while it does include some fairly run-of-the-mill Dutch pictures, there are also a number of works of real quality. The star is undoubtedly the great Ruisdael, *The Banks of a River*, currently on loan to the National Gallery of Scotland. It is an early work by the artist, but it shows his talent already fully formed and is one of the finest paintings by Ruisdael in any British public collection. Among the other outstanding Dutch works, the remarkable picture by Ten Oever of bathers in the evening sun with the town of Zwolle in the background is a memorable and very unusual picture which has made an impact at several exhibitions of Dutch landscape painting in recent years, most notably at the major exhibition at the Rijksmuseum in 1988, *Masters of Seventeenth Century Dutch Landscape Painting*. Likewise when *The Forest Glade* by Pynacker was shown at the definitive Pynacker exhibition at the Sterling & Francine Clark Art Institute, Massachusetts, in 1994 it looked very good indeed in the company of its peers. *The Cavalcade* by van der Meulen is unique in British public collections although the painter, who worked at the court of Louis XIV, is well represented in the Louvre. *Ships in a Calm* by Willem van der Velde and *The Squall* by Backhuysen are both good examples of the Dutch art of seascape. There are a number of other Dutch paintings of quality such as *Halt at a Winehouse Door* by Karel du Jardin, and although it is Flemish and not Dutch, the painting by David Teniers the Younger, *Peasants Playing Bowls*, is also widely recognised as a very fine example of the artist's work. Its importance as a work that marks the beginning of the artist's mature style was demonstrated at a major exhibition in Antwerp in 1991.

As well as the Dutch pictures, there is also a group of Italian paintings. There are good examples of work by both Gaspard Poussin and Salvator Rosa. The landscape with a bather attributed to Domenichino is also a picture of great quality. At the moment it is not clear who the artist is, but the picture certainly belongs to the period in the 1620s or '30s in Rome when the classical style of landscape was first formed by Domenichino and his immediate followers, shaping the art ever since.

Although the authorship of this picture does still remain a mystery, the publication of this catalogue has provided an opportunity to reconsider some earlier attributions and to take account of new scholarship in the case of a number of works in the collection. The *Madonna and Child with St Catherine*, for instance, traditionally attributed to Titian, turns out to be a variation on a composition by his little known elder brother. But not all this kind of reattribution has resulted in downgrading pictures. It was suggested by Christopher Wright for example in his survey of Dutch paintings in British collections that the two paintings by Hobbema, which have for long been treated as copies, or even in the case of *A Woody Lane, with a thatched Cottage and a Pool*, as actual fakes, do in fact have a reasonable claim to be autograph.

Although there are fewer sculptures than paintings in the Torrie Collection, they do include some of the most important works. Some of these, like the small imitation classical bronzes, or the group of bronze vases by Zoffoli, were no doubt really no more than fashionable furnishings, but there are enough more substantial works to suggest that Sir James did have an independent taste for sculpture. Some of the other smaller bronzes are now recognised as works of some quality however, for instance the small *Mercury* after Giambologna and the copies of *Dawn* and *Night,* two of Michelangelo's figures in the Medici Chapel in Florence, which are now thought to be by the Susini workshop.

The two outstanding sculptures are, however, the *Ecorché Horse* formerly attributed to Giambologna and the group of *Cain and Abel* by Adriaen de Vries. In 1804 Sir James apparently tried to sell the horse and so it seems to have been an early acquisition. Closely related to studies of horses made by Leonardo, it is a very beautiful and highly unusual object. The same is true of the sculpture by de Vries. Exhibited in the major de Vries exhibition in Holland, Sweden and the US in 1998–9 it was clearly established as one of the most vivid of his works of the period. It was unusual in the early nineteenth century to value the kind of expressive force that this work displays. The neoclassical calm of Ponçet's *Venus* is more typical of contemporary taste in sculpture. Both the former works demonstrate the independence of Sir James's taste therefore, but they may however also link his early interest in sculpture with the work of his contemporary and fellow pupil of David Allan, the surgeon Charles Bell. Bell's main contribution to science was his study of the nervous system, but his book *The Anatomy of Expression,* published in 1806, was a very important and influential text for artists at the time, notably for David Wilkie for instance. Both these sculptures find an echo in Bell's study of expression carried out in Edinburgh in the first years of the nineteenth century, just at the moment when Sir James may have acquired the bronze horse, and so they may link his interest in art to some of the most advanced contemporary thinking in Scotland.

Sir James Erskine died in 1825. On the 10th April 1824

he had drawn up his will leaving the greater part of his collection to the University of Edinburgh. Later interpretation of his will by the Court of Session has established that this was not an outright bequest but that the University holds the collection in trust and that the University Court is one of three trustees. The other two, named in the will are the Sheriff of Midlothian and the Lord Provost of Edinburgh. Be that as it may, Sir James's intention, declared in his will, was 'to lay the foundation of a Gallery for the encouragement of the Fine Arts.' This may have been prompted by the recent establishment of the National Gallery in London and the wish to establish a similar institution for Scotland in Edinburgh. Several great collectors like Sir George Beaumont played an important part in setting up the new National Gallery in London and Sir James may well have seen his own role in Scotland as similar. It is not clear why he did not think that the Institution for the Promotion of the Fine Arts in Scotland was a suitable destination for his collection. It had recently been established in Edinburgh, and indeed he had lent a number of works to its first exhibition. There were, however, also good reasons for choosing the University. Only a few years earlier the Hunterian Museum in Glasgow University, housing William Hunter's great bequest, had become Scotland's first public museum. Edinburgh University's own association with the fine arts was however already of long standing too. It began with the Academy of St Luke housed in the College in 1729 and continued with the provision of the teaching of drawing for surgeons under Alexander Munro 'Primus'. Later the Trustees Academy was housed in the College buildings for much of the eighteenth century. It was there, as we have seen, that Sir James's own teacher, David Allan, had been master. This direct connection with the visual arts ceased early in the nineteenth century. Nevertheless it left the University with the ambition to play a role in the fine arts that was eventually realised with the establishment of the Fine Art chair many years later.

The collection eventually came to the University on the death of his brother, John Drummond Erskine, in 1836. Sir James's will specified that the University was to inherit the works that were at the time of his death in his London house. This proved difficult to establish and the task of working out what was where was given to Andrew Wilson and William Playfair. The involvement of Playair in this suggests that he may have been instrumental in persuading Sir James to choose the University as his beneficiary as at the time that his will was drawn up, Playfair was engaged on commissioning the University's new building, now known as Old College. It may well have seemed that there would be an opportunity to create a suitable space in it to house the collection. In the event, when it came to the University it was displayed on the Library staircase. This proved unsuitable and in 1844 the whole collection was loaned to the Royal Institution. (It had been granted its Royal Charter shortly after Sir James's death.) This transfer was not carried out without protest however and provoked heated discussions in the University Senatus. Neverthless on the foundation of the National Gallery of Scotland, the collection passed on to it. The condition of this loan was always that the identity of the collection should be preserved. Gradually as the National Gallery's own holdings grew this became more and more difficult and the larger part of the Torrie Collection was kept in store. Meanwhile the University did not lose sight of its ownership and the entire Torrie Collection was listed annually in the University Calendar along with the growing collection of portraits and portrait busts until the 1920s. In the early 1930s, Herbert Read as Professor of Fine Art brought some small items of the Torrie Collection back into the University. Twenty years later, his successor David Talbot Rice, brought back the bulk of the collection and displayed it in Adam House. It was then transferred to the Talbot Rice Gallery. In 1983 the remaining works were brought there from the National Gallery and so for the first time for a century the collection was displayed once again in its entirety.

Circle of Giovanni da Bologna (Jean de Boulogne) known as Giambologna

B. DOUAI 1529 – D. FLORENCE 1608

Giambologna trained in Flanders with sculptor Jacques du Broeuq. In 1550 he set out for Rome and on his return journey was persuaded to stay in Florence. Thereafter he carried out a series of monumental projects for the Medici and became the most celebrated and influential sculptor after Michelangelo. In his work he combined the formal lessons of Michelangelo's sculpture with the elegance of newly discovered Roman and Hellenistic works. His own work was widely disseminated through small copies. Some of these originated in his studio, both during his lifetime and subsequentlly. But he also had a habit of making small cabinet sculptures which were much sought after by collectors throughout Europe.

Anatomical Figure of a Horse (ecorché)

Bronze, black patina, many casting flaws
h.90.2 cm · EU cat.643

This is a version of a bronze horse formerly in the Villa Mattei, Rome, although, it has been argued, it cannot be the actual Mattei horse which was still in Italy in 1808. (John Winter, *Valadier: Three Generations of Roman Goldsmiths*, Artemis, London, 1991) Sir James Erskine already owned this horse by then as he made an attempt to sell it in 1804. Three other versions of the horse are known. One is in the Palazzo Vecchio in Florence, another in the Springfield Museum of Fine Arts, Massachusets and the third in a private collection.

In pose and attitude, the horse is a flayed version of the horse in the statue of Marcus Aurelius on the Capitoline. Traditionally it has always been thought that it originated in the studio of Giambologna and was connected in some way with the equestrian statue of Duke Cosimo I which was commissioned in 1587 and completed in 1594.

The original écorché horse is most likely to have been made as a finished object in wax which can be coloured and so can carry much more anatomical information than bronze. Indeed, lacking that information, bronze actually makes little sense as a material for an écorché figure. If this is so, then none of the bronze versions is truly primary. Some of the earliest known écorchés were made in wax in Giambologna's studio. One of his assistants, Pietro Francavilla, is shown holding an écorché in an anonymous portrait dated 1576. Bronze casts of this and two other écorché figures by him also survive.

These early écorchés were all of the human figure. However Baldinucci states that in 1587 Giambologna was ordered to start work for the commission by making studies of the horse. The figure was to come later. A scientific study of a horse's anatomy would be an appropriate response to that command. Baldinucci also adds that Lodovico Carde, called Il Cigoli, and Gregorio Pagani were invited to assist with these studies and that they contributed drawings, some of which he had seen. Cigoli's involvement is of particular interest here as he was celebrated for his study of anatomy. He made himself ill studying cadavers in his youth and later collaborated in actual dissections with the celebrated Flemish anatomist Teodoro Marion. He was also a pioneer in making wax écorché figures. One made by him survives in

13

the Bargello. He was a friend of Galileo and his interest in exact scientific observation and its role in art is reflected in his use of Galileo's observation of the moon in his fresco of the Immaculate Conception in Santa Maria Maggiore.

If he had access to them, Leonardo's studies of horses would however also have been of great interest to Giambologna at this point. There is a striking similarity between the écorché horse and some of Leonardo's drawings. Leonardo's preoccupation with the idea of the equestrian monument was also well known and the immediate precedent for Giambologna's own project was in fact Leonardo's last attempt to realise this ambition, the Trivulzio monument destined for Florence.

A scientific interest in anatomy similar to that shown by Il Cigoli is also reflected in the earliest evidence for the horse's existence, or at least, perhaps, the existence of its wax original. This was the model for three plates in Carlo Ruini's book *Dell Anatomia et dell Infirmita dell Cavallo* published in Bologna in 1598. It is conceivable that the original model was made for Ruini, but these three plates are different in character from all the others in the book which look as though they originated in actual dissections. Also, if he had gone to the expense of having a flayed model made, Ruini would surely have used it more extensively. It seems more likely that he took advantage of an existing anatomical study made by an artist of reputation. The argument put forward by Bent Sørensen in *Apollo* (August 2002) that the bronze versions derive from the plates in Ruini is untenable. The three plates are clearly three different views of an existing three dimensional object which has a distinctly sculptural character.

The left foreleg and right rear leg of the Torrie horse were broken in casting or at some later date and repaired with iron bolts. The same flaw in the rear leg appears in the version of the horse in Florence. The tip of the right ear of the Torrie horse is missing. There is a casting defect in the rear right hoof made up in bronze and lead and many other small flaws and nail holes have been left unplugged. Both these horses have a black patina. In the Florence horse this is very crudely applied. The common flaw and the rather rough, casual condition of both horses, which is even more marked in the Florence horse, suggests that they were cast at the same time and that they were made for studio use rather than as art objects for collectors. That the model was extensively used as a study object has been demonstrated by Bent Sørensen.

These two casts may therefore have been from a wax original made as a study for Giambologna's large equestrian monument. Perhaps this original was by Il Cigoli. It may be argued that as Baldinucci gives a detailed account of the making of the monument and also greatly admired Il Cigoli, if the écorché horse had been made by him, he would have mentioned it; but Baldinucci was writing a century later. It is also significant that the grounds for his admiration were what he saw as Il Cigoli's revival of a true classiscism based on the study of nature. Indeed he speaks of Il Cigoli very much as Bellori speaks of Annibale Carracci and the two painters did in fact collaborate in Rome. It is its compound of scientific naturalism and classic form that is so striking in the horse.

If either the Florence horse or the Torrie horse was in fact the one from the Villa Mattei, and neither has an early provenance, these two casts would have been made before 1707 when the Mattei horse is first recorded. Of the two other versions of the horse the one in a private collection is much more elegant and has a brown, highy polished patina and a high finish. It seems likely to be an eighteenth-century copy of the Villa Mattei horse by the sculptor Luigi Valadier. The Springfield horse is different again. It lacks the high finish of Valadier, but is also less delicate in its modelling than the other two horses.

In 1984 a cast was made from the Torrie horse by the Swiss Foundry, Mario Pastori, and an edition was undertaken by Cyril Humphris. The project ran into difficulties after the death of Pastori and the edition was never completed. The initial cast however was bought by the Breeder's Cup organisation and is installed in their headquarters in Lexington, Kentucky. A small copy of the horse is given as the trophy to the winners of the race.

EXHIBITED: *Giambologna: Sculptor to the Medici* 1978, National Museum of Scotland; V.&A. 1978; *Horses of St. Marks c.*1980, R.A. London. (Prior to 1976 the Horse was displayed in the entrance hall of the N.G.S.)

Adrian de Vries

B. THE HAGUE *c.*1555/6 — D. PRAGUE 1626

The most celebrated sculptor in Europe after the death of Giambologna, De Vries may have trained as a goldsmith in the Hague, but possibly also as a sculptor on a larger scale in Delft with sculptor Willem van Tetrode, a pupil of Benvenuto Cellini. De Vries was in Florence in the studio of Giambologna by 1581, when indeed he is described as a goldsmith. In 1586 he left Florence for Milan to work on the monumental High Altar for the Escorial with Pompeo Leoni. In 1587 or '88 he moved to Turin to work for the Duke of Savoy. He then went to Prague from 1589–1594, loaned by the Duke of Savoy to Emperor Rudolf II, but still nominally on the duke's payroll. He returned to the Hague in the latter year and was in Rome again from 1595–6. In 1596 he went to Augsburg where he made two monumental fountains, but in 1601 he returned to Prague as King's sculptor, a very distinguished position close to the Emperor. After Rudolf's death in 1612 he remained in Prague receiving commissions from all over Europe including an important commission from Sweden's Christian IV for Drottningholm Palace.

Cain and Abel, 1612

Bronze, h.75 cm, inscribed 'Adrianus Fries
Hagiensis Batavus f.1612'

EU cat.645

One of only three works by de Vries in Britain
and one of the most important in the Torrie
Collection. The subject was originally called
Samson Slaying the Philistines, but is in fact *Cain and
Abel* and the composition is based on Giambologna's large group of that subject now in the
V&A., itself in turn based on a work by
Michelangelo. The contrast between de Vries's
work and that of his master is marked however,
not just in the much greater liveliness of the
composition, but also in the vivid finish.Perhaps
in reaction to Giambologna's elegance and high
finish, de Vries returned to study Michelangelo's
expressive power and cultivated spontaneity, or in
the Italian term *sprezzatura*, in his own work. This
is a particularly fine example of this quality. The
direct casting method he favoured, as it suited
this approach, did not allow multiple copies, a
further contrast with Giambologna. A gilded
replica was made of this composition however
and is dated 1622 (National Museum, Copenha-
gen). *Cain and Abel* was made for Emperor
Rudolph II and the subject has been shown
(*Adrian de Vries, Imperial Sculptor*) to have a direct
personal significance for the Emperor who spent
the last six years of his life engaged in fratricidal
strife with his brother Matthias. The struggle
eventually led to the occupation of Prague by
Matthias's troops in March 1611, just at the
moment when the sculpture is likely to have been
conceived. Rudolf was held captive by his brother
in Hradcany Castle, and for the last year of his
life – he died in January 1612 – Rudolf was an
Emperor without an empire. The bronze was
presumably looted from Prague by the troops of
Gustavus Adolphus in 1648. If that was so, then it
is likely it was in the collection of Queen
Christina of Sweden. There is no record of this
however, nor of its subsequent history; nor is
there any record of where or when it was
acquired by Sir James Erskine. Considering its
eventual appearance in Scotland, it is of interest
that a plaster cast of the bronze appears to have
been in the collection of Sir John Medina who
based a painting of the same subject on it. (Sir
John Clerk of Penicuik.)

EXHIBITED: *Prague 1600: Art and Culture at the
Court of Rudolph II* 1988–89, Kunsthistorisches
Museum, Vienna; *Adrian de Vries, Imperial Sculptor*
1998–99, Rijksmuseum, National Museum
Stockholm, and Getty Museum, Los Angeles

Ludolf Backhuyzen

B. EMDEN 1631 — D. AMSTERDAM 1708

Backhuyzen was the outstanding seascapist in
the Netherlands after the two William van de
Veldes moved to England *c*.1673. He was a pupil
of Hendrik Drubbels and was influenced by
William van de Velde the Younger. His work was
popular and much imitated.

A Squall: A lugger running into harbour

Oil on canvas · 46.4 × 61 cm
Signed 'L.Backhuyzen' · EU cat.701
Sir James Erskine, 1823, lists 'Backhuysen –
A Brisk Gale'. HdeG no.199
EXHIBITED: Edinburgh Institution 1819, lent Sir
James Erskine; RI Edinburgh 1830, lent John
Erskine.

Karel du Jardin

PROBABLY B. AMSTERDAM 1622 –
D. VENICE 1678

Du Jardin studied under Berchem before 1643. He was probably in Rome during late 1640s, was in Amsterdam in 1652 and then in Paris 1650–52. He became a guild painter at The Hague in 1656. He was in Amsterdam again in 1659 and returned to Italy in 1675 moving to Venice, where he died, in 1678. He was a versatile painter, but is best known for his Italianate pastoral scenes.

Halt at a Winehouse Door, 1675–78

Oil on canvas · 81 × 89.6 cm · EU cat.719

This work is one of a group of late landscapes painted in Italy 1675–78. Waagen thought that the tone of the distance at the horizon was 'somewhat too uniformly insipid', whereas HdG was altogether more disparaging. J. Kilian, however, relates this picture both in composition and theme to a painting currently in Turin, *Extensive Landscape with Travellers Halted for Refreshment at an Inn* by Du Jardin (J. Lloyd Williams, *Dutch Art & Scotland*). HdeG no 236 and listed as du Jardin by Christopher Wright (Birmingham 1989)

EXHIBITED: Edinburgh Institution 1819, lent by Sir James Erskine; *Le paysage hollandais au XVIII*, Orangerie Paris, 1950–51; *Nederlandse 17 Eeuwse Italianiserende Landschaapschilders*, Centraal Museum, Utrecht, 1965; *Dutch Art and Scotland – A Reflection of Taste*, NGS, Edinburgh 1992

Pieter van der Leeuw

B. DORDRECHT 1647 — D. 1679

Leeuw specialized in landscapes with cattle in
the manner of Adriaen van de Velde. He
became a member of the Dordrecht Guild of
St. Luke in 1669 and Regent in 1678. His works
are rare, though often signed and dated. They
are smoother and more detailed than those of
van de Velde to which they are otherwise
comparable.

Landscape with Cattle and Figures

Oil on canvas · 82.5 × 105.5 cm
signed and dated 'P.van der Leeuw 1674'
EU cat.722

In spite of the signature and date this picture
was ascribed to Adriaen van de Velde until 1893.
Listed as by van der Leeuw by Christopher
Wright (Birmingham 1989)

Jan Lievens

B. LEYDEN 1607 – D. ANTWERP? 1674

Lievens studied with Pieter Lastman, *c.*1617–19. He was a close friend of Rembrandt, probably sharing a Leyden studio and models with him *c.*1625–31. His works of this period are often confused with Rembrandt's. He visited England *c.*1631–35, where he was influenced by Van Dyck, and was in Antwerp 1635–44 where he was influenced by Rubens and Brouwer and experimented with landscape painting. He returned to Amsterdam in 1644.

A Wooded Walk

Oil on canvas · 51.5 × 70.5 cm
*c.*1650 · EU cat.723

This painting is one of a group of unusual, moody landscapes inspired by Brouwer. The attribution would be doubtful if there were not a closely related picture in Berlin which is signed. Listed as by Lievens by Christopher Wright (Birmingham 1989).

EXHIBITED: RI Edinburgh 1830 as Rembrandt, lent John Erskine; Herzog Anton Ulrich Museum, Brunswick 1979

Adam Frans Van der Meulen

B. BRUSSELS 1632 — D. PARIS 1690

Van der Meulen was invited to Paris by Colbert
through Charles le Brun to depict the martial
successes of Louis XIV. He became a member of
the French Academy in 1673.

A Cavalcade

Oil on canvas · 60.5 × 83 cm
signed 'V Meulen Fc' · EU cat.725

This painting is a typical subject for Van der
Meulen, a progress of Louis XIV, and is similar
to one in Dresden entitled *Ausfahrt Konig Ludwig
nach Vincennes*. The king himself is clearly
identifiable seated in his carriage. He is the only
passenger wearing a hat while on either side his
attendants face outwards towards the crowd.

Hendrick ten Oever

B. ZWOLLE 1639 – D. 1716

Ten Oever may have studied in Zwolle before moving to Amsterdam where he was a pupil of his cousin Cornelis de Bie shortly after 1657. He returned to Zwolle in 1664 painted portraits, landscapes and decorative works, and is the best known Zwolle artist. His landscapes were influenced by Cuyp.

Canal Landscape with Figures Bathing

Oil on canvas · 66.7 × 87 cm

1673 signed 'H ten Oever 1675' · EU cat.727

Sir James Erskine, 1823, lists 'Cuyp – Bathers'. In this painting a distant view of Zwolle is on the horizon. One of the very few signed and dated works by this artist, it was originally assigned to Cuyp in the Torrie Catalogues and to Jan Ossenbeck in the NGS. catalogues until 1884, when the signature was read correctly. Ten Oever did another version of the composition with clothed figures the following year. No particular significance can be attached to the subject matter. The subject of men bathing occurs again from time to time in Dutch painting of the period. The picture was bought by Sir James Erskine in 1822 from Siegfried Bendixen. Listed as by Ten Oever by Christopher Wright (Birmingham 1989)

EXHIBITED: RI Edinburgh, 1830 as Cuyp, lent by John Erskine; Zwolle 1957; *Masters of Seventeenth Century Dutch Landscape Painting*', 1988, Rijksmuseum, Amsterdam; *Dutch Art in the Seventeenth Century: Images of a Golden Age in British Collections*, 1990, Birmingham Museum & Art Gallery; *Dutch Art & Scotland: A Reflection of Taste* 1992, NGS; *Paysages, paysans*, 1994, Bibliotheque Nationale de France, Paris; *The Golden Age of Dutch Landscape Painting*, 1995, Museo de Arte Thyssen-Bornemisza, Madrid.

Gaspard Poussin
(Gaspard Dughet)

B. ROME OF FRENCH PARENTS 1615 —
D. ROME 1675

Poussin was a landscapist and was a pupil of his
brother-in-law Nicolas Poussin in 1630–31. He
was also influenced by Claude. He travelled
round Italy, but worked mainly in Rome. His
work was in vogue in 18th c. and his romantic
effects were much imitated, influencing the
picturesque movement in Britain.

A Land Storm

Oil on canvas · 53 × 79 cm · EU cat.728

Another version or copy of this picture was on
sale in Rome in 1974, but the Torrie picture may
be the one formerly in the Altieri Palace
Collection, Rome.

Giulio Cesare Procaccini

B. BOLOGNA 1574 — D. MILAN 1626

Procaccini was a pupil of his father Ercole. He was first active as a sculptor in Milan then in the same city as a painter. Up to *c.*1616 he was influenced mainly by Parmesan artists.

Dead Christ with Angels

Oil on paper laid on wood · panel, 28 × 43 cm
*c.*1615–16 · EU cat.729

This work is a fine bozzetto, or colour modello, for the lunette of the *Dead Christ with Angels* now in the sacristy of Sant Angelo, Milan, which formerly decorated the doorway separating two cloisters of Sant Angelo. M. Valsecchi, (*Il seicento lombardo: catalogo dei dipinti e delle sculture*, Milan, 1973, p.44, no.94.) gives the date of 1615–16, and he points out compositional differences from the final lunette design. Michael Bury ("Procaccini's 'Dead Christ'; placing an unusual composition in context", *Apollo*, CXXXIII, 1991, pp.327–31) interprets these changes as concerned with meaning, rather than purely a design decision. He suggests that the alterations embody changes in the emotional and theologi-cal content: the finished lunette spells out the hope for salvation represented by Christ's sacrifice and the iconographic inclusion of more angel figures relates to the church's true name, S. Maria degli Angeli.

EXHIBITED: *Il Seicento Lombardo*, Milan 1973

Salvator Rosa

B. NAPLES 1615 – D. ROME 1673

Rosa studied with Ribera in Naples, then went to Rome 1635 and achieved success as a landscapist. His poetic treatment of nature and his vision of a rugged wilderness, usually inhabited by bandits, was immensely popular with 18th and 19th c. British collectors and was a formative influence on picturesque taste.

Rocky Landscape with Figures

Oil on canvas · 51 × 92 cm · EU cat.732

Sir James Erskine, 1823, lists 'Salvator Rosa – A Mountainous and rocky landscape ... some figures in the foreground'. This picture is perhaps related to *Mountain Landscape and a Man Bathing*, City of Southampton Gallery.

Adam Pynacker

B. PIJNAKKER NEAR DELFT
c.1620 – D. 1673

Pynacker probably worked in Italy in his early career, but is recorded in Delft 1649–51. He was later in Lenzen and Schiedam and settled in Amsterdam *c*.1661.

A Forest Glade

Oil on canvas · 81.2 × 90 cm
signed indistinctly *A. Pynacker* · EU cat.730

Harwood (*A Golden Harvest: Paintings of Adam Pynacker*) dates this picture to about 1657, noting that it includes one of the first instances of Pynacker's recurring motif of a gnarled decaying birch tree stump, and also the foliage of wild cabbage in the foreground. *A Forest Glade* may have had a companion work, but this has been lost. (J.Lloyd Williams, *Dutch Art & Scotland*). The picture was probably sold in Paris by Pierre de Grandpré and bought by A. de la Hante and then included in a sale of the latter's pictures by Philips in London on June 2 1814.(Harwood) This is presumably when Sir James Erskine acquired it. Listed as by Pynacker by Christopher Wright (Birmingham 1989)

EXHIBITED: *Dutch Art in the Seventeenth Century: Images of a Golden Age in British Collections*, 1990, Birmingham Museum & Art Gallery; *Reflections on Italy'* R.L.Feigen & Co. 1991, London; *Dutch Art & Scotland; A Reflection of Taste*, 1992, NGS; *A Golden Harvest: Paintings of Adam Pynacker*, 1994, Sterling & Francine Clark Art Institute, Massachusetts.

Jan Steen

B. LEYDEN 1626 — D. 1679

Steen worked at Leyden, the Hague and Haarlem. He was a prolific and inventive painter of genre scenes.

The Doctor's Visit

Oil on canvas · 57.2 × 71.1 cm
signed J.Steen · EU cat.738

This work is dateable c.1660 and relates to a painting of the same subject in the Mauritshuis, the Hague. HdG (*Oud Holland*, 1893, p.129) thought it a copy, but there is no reason to suppose it is not an autograph work, if in poor condition. It is not a straightforward copy of the Mauritshuis picture, but an independent version of the same subject. There are considerable differences between them. The main figures are closely similar, but they are differently placed within the picture space. There are also only three figures in the Mauritshuis version, but in this picture a fourth figure looks in from a window on the right which replaces an arched door. In the Mauritshuis picture the colour is different. The bed curtain is blue, not red as

here, and the woman wears a light red dress, not a dark red velvet jacket and gold skirt as she does in this picture. The table is also on the right of the picture, not as here on the left where its structure is also partly visible beneath the carpet. Indeed the artist's signature is on the cross bar. In the Torrrie picture an inquisitive black and white dog occupies the middle of the foreground, but it does not appear in the Mauritshuis painting. The painting on the wall in the latter picture seems to represent the battle of the Lapiths and Centaurs; certainly it is a scene of violence. In the Torrie picture only part of the equivalent painting on the wall is visible, but it is very different and clearly represents two lovers in an embrace. There is nothing really to identify them as Venus and Adonis, as suggested by Wright, however (Birmingham 1989). The patient appears to be in the throes of fever until we realise that she is sick with love – her lover can just be seen through the window in the background. Wright also lists the picture as by Steen (Birmingham 1989). Another version of this composition also exists in an English private collection.

EXHIBITED: *Dutch Art in the Seventeenth Century: Images of a Golden Age in British Collections*, 1989, Birmingham Museum & Art Gallery

David Teniers the Younger

B. ANTWERP 1610 — D. BRUSSELS 1690

Teniers studied under his father and was influenced by Rubens and Brouwer. In 1651 he was established as Court Painter at Brussels.

Peasants playing Bowls

Oil on wood · 35 × 57.2 cm · signed D. Teniers
EU cat.739

Painted in the mid–1630s (Margret Klinger, *David Teniers de Jonge*, Antwerp 1991, no.15) this is an important early work. It is the first and, especially in the sharpness of observation of the figures, in some ways it is the finest example of the subject of peasants playing bowls that Teniers repeated a number of times (for example in a painting in the Los Angeles County Museum). The figures show the influence of Brouwer, but the picture also shows the emergence of Teniers's distinctive style of landscape painting. This is clearly influenced by the monochrome

landscapes of Jan van Goyen and Peter de Molijn, but is already independent. Sir James Erskine, 1823, lists 'Teniers, ditto a Copy' which seems to describe this picture and no.740 below, p.40.

Exhibited, *Pictures for Scotland*, NGS, Edinburgh 1972; *David Teniers de Jonge*, Koninklijk Museum voor Schonen Kunsten, Antwerp 1991, no.15

William van de Velde the younger

B. LEYDEN 1633 — D. GREENWICH, ENGLAND 1707

Van der Velde was a pupil and collaborator of his father, Willem van de Velde the Elder. He moved to England in 1672 where he and his father were both employed by Charles II in 1674 and continued to be employed by the court thereafter.

Fishing Boats in a Calm

Oil on canvas · 41.9 × 56.2 cm
Signed W. V. Velde 1658 · EU cat.744

'Such marine scenes as this have long collected by the Scots, whose own boats were often built by the Dutch.' (Lloyd-Williams *Dutch Art & Scotland; A Reflection of Taste*) HdeG no.190, also listed as by Willem van der Velde (Birmingham 1989).

EXHIBITED: *Dutch Art & Scotland; A Reflection of Taste* 1992, NGS.

Studio of Paolo Veronese

B. VERONA 1528 — D. VENICE 1588

Venus and Adonis

Oil on canvas · 56 × 82 cm · EU cat.745

A communication to Sir James Erskine from Geo.Simpson, dated 1820, invoices £18:18 'To cleaning, lining and repairing a Capital Picture of Venus and Adonis with Cupids and Dogs. In very bad condition. By P. Veronese'. Two inches along the top and half an inch along the bottom are later additions. This is a good copy of an untraced original from the Dupille sale in Paris 1780, engraved by Ravenet in 1742. At least two other copies are known. Fiocco identifies it as by Parrasio Micheli (*Paolo Veronese* 1934).

Richard Wilson

B. MONTGOMERYSHIRE 1713 — D. MOLD 1782

Wilson went to London in the 1740s as a
portrait painter, but turned to landscape when
he travelled in Italy 1750–57. There he was
influenced by Zuccarelli, whom he knew
personally, and by C.J. Vernet.

An Italian Landscape

Oil on canvas · 51.5 × 73 cm

c.1751 · EU cat.746

This is an early work probably painted in Italy
and is closely related to a painting which Wilson
gave to Zuccarelli in 1751.

EXHIBITED: Probably Edinburgh Institution
1819, lent by Sir James Erskine and in 1830 lent
by Sir John Erskine; *Fontane und die Bildende Kunst*
1998–99, Staatlichte Museum, Berlin & Neue
Pinacothek, Munich

COMPLETE CATALOGUE OF THE TORRIE COLLECTION

ABBREVIATIONS

Birmingham 1989: *Dutch Art in the Seventeenth Century: Images of a Golden Age in British Collections*, 1989, Birmingham Museum & Art Gallery

HdG: Hoofstede de Groot, *A Catalogue Raisonné of the Works of the most eminent Dutch Painters of the Seventeenth Century*, 10 Vols (London 1908–28)

NGS: National Gallery of Scotland

RI: Royal Institution for the Promotion of the Fine Arts in Scotland

Waagen: G. F. Waagen, *Treasures of Art in Great Britain*, 3 vols, and Supplement (London 1854–7)

PAINTINGS

Ludolf Backhuyzen

SEE PAGE 18

Claes Pietersz Berchem

B. HAARLEM 1620 – D. AMSTERDAM 1683

Berchem was the son and pupil of still-life painter Pieter Claesz. Berchem and entered the Haarlem Guild in 1642. He was in Italy from 1642–5 and latterly lived in Amsterdam 1677–83. His arcadian pastoral scenes of the Roman Campagna were very popular in France in the 18th c.

Cattle in a Stream, with a Herd Boy Resting

Oil on wood · 25 × 31 cm
Signed 'Berchem' · EU cat.702
EXHIBITED: probably Edinburgh Institution 1819, lent by Sir James Erskine

A Herdsman Driving Cattle down a Lane

Oil on wood · 24 × 30.5 cm
Inscribed 'Berchem' · EU cat.703
This may be by an imitator of Berchem as HdG suspected (HdG IX, *Oud Holland*, German edition, 481)

Andries Both
A Rocky Landscape with Figures, Sunset

Andries Both

B. UTRECHT 1612 – D. VENICE 1641

Like his more famous younger brother Jan (see below 705 & 706), Andries Both was a pupil of Bloemart in Utrecht. He went to in Italy in 1632 and stayed in Rome until 1641. He went to Venice in 1641 where he was drowned in an accident. The brothers' Italianate landscapes were were much imitated in Holland.

A Rocky Landscape with Figures, Sunset

Oil on canvas · 47 × 57.5 cm · EU cat.704

Sir James Erskine 1823, lists 'Both – A Mountainous Landscape'. Earlier catalogues have questioned the authenticity of this picture. Christopher Wright (Birmingham 1989) however lists it as by Andries Both.

Claes Pietersz Berchem
A Herdsman Driving Cattle down a Lane

Jan Both
Landscape with Figures

Jan Both

B. UTRECHT 1618/22 — D. UTRECHT 1652

Jan Both was the most gifted of the Dutch 17th c. Italianate landscapists. He trained with his father and with Bloemaert and was in Italy with his brother *c*.1637–1641. He was elected President of the Guild of Painters in Utrecht 1649. He was much influenced by the landscapes of Claude Lorraine and his scenes of travellers in wooded mountain landscapes and evocatively lit Roman ruins highly were esteemed in the 18th c.

Landscape with Figures

Oil on canvas · 102 × 106 cm
Signed 'J. Both' · EU cat.705

Sir James Erskine, 1823, lists 'Both – a warm landscape with a large tree in the centre, a lake in the distance and high ground to the left –

Figures by Andrew'. Christopher Wright (Birmingham 1989) lists both this and no.706 below as by Jan Both.

Landscape with Mounted Figures

Oil on wood · 41 × 70.5 cm · EU cat.706

Jacques Courtois (Il Borgognone)

B. ST.HIPPOLYTE, FRANCHE
COMTÉ 1621 — D. ROME 1676

Courtois trained under his father, but entered the army aged 15 and served for 3 years. On settling in Rome he first painted religious subjects, but then turned to what was to be his forté, battle-pieces, for which he became renowned. Towards the end of his life he joined the Jesuit order.

Skirmish

Oil on canvas · 34 × 57 cm
EU cat.707, pair to no.708

This, and no.708 below, are typical of Il Borgognone's battle pictures.

Skirmish

Oil on canvas · 34 × 57 cm
EU cat.708, pair to no.707

Jacques Courtois (Il Borgognone)
Skirmish

Jacques Courtois (Il Borgognone)
Skirmish

Jan Both
Landscape with Mounted Figures

Domenico Zampieri, called Domenichino

B. BOLOGNA 1581 — D. NAPLES 1641

Domenichino studied under the Carracci in Bologna and followed Albani to Rome after 1600, where he became principal assistant to Annibale Carracci in the fresco decoration of the Farnese Palace. Domenichino was in Bologna again, 1619–1621, and then returned once more to Rome at the invitation of Pope Gregory XV to be his principal architect. From 1624–28 he worked on the frescoes in the choir of S.Andrea della Valle. In 1630 he was invited to Naples to decorate the Del Tesoro Chapel and died in Naples. Domenichino's style belongs very much in the classical tradition established by Annibale Carracci. He was however also one of the pioneers of landscape painting in Rome.

A Bather

Oil on canvas · 43 × 53 cm · EU cat.710

The attribution of this picture to Domenichino is traditional. It is certainly a picture of great quality from early seventeenth century Rome and it does have some of the characteristics of his approach to landscape.

After Domenichino
Martyrdom of St Andrew

After Domenichino
Martyrdom of St Andrew

Oil on canvas · 33 × 43 cm · EU cat.709
Sir James Erskine, 1823, lists 'after Domenichino – Martyrdom of St. Andrew'.

This painting is a late 17th/ early 18th c. copy after an engraving of Domenichino's fresco of this subject on the vault of S. Andrea della Valle, in Rome.

Giovanni Ghisolfi

B. MILAN 1632 — D. MILAN 1683

Ghisolfi was a Milanese aristocrat and pupil of Salvator Rosa. He painted historical, decorative and architectural subjects.

Architectural Composition of Ruins

Oil on canvas · 97 × 118 cm
Signed with a monogram I.S. · EU cat.712, pair to no.713

Catalogued as Ghisolfi on grounds of subject and its relationship to no.713. The monogram 'I.S.' has thrown doubt on this attribution and Jean Nicholas Servandony (1695–1766) has been suggested as author of the picture.

Ruins and Figures

Oil on canvas · 97 × 118 cm · EU cat.713
Pair to no.712

Domenico Zampieri, called Domenichino
A Bather

Jean Baptiste Greuze
Interior of a Cottage

Jean Baptiste Greuze

B. TOURNUS NEAR MACON 1725 –
D. PARIS 1805

Greuze left the studio of a provincial painter in Lyons and settled in Paris *c*.1750. In 1755 he made his name in the Salon with *La Lecture de Bible*, a work profoundly influenced by Dutch and Flemish 17th c. genre painting, then very popular in France. His moralising sentimental style was much admired by Diderot.

Interior of a Cottage

Oil on canvas · 63.2 × 80.6 cm
signed 'J.B.Greuze.' · EU cat.715

This is a more straightforward re-interpretation of a Dutch 17th c. genre theme than Greuze's more famous didactic subjects.

Meindert Hobbema

B. AMSTERDAM 1638 – D. 1709

Hobbema was a pupil and friend of Jacob van Ruisdael, but his work was more picturesque and was very fashionable in the eighteenth century.

A Woody Lane, with a Thatched Cottage and a Pool

Oil on wood · 51.4 × 90.8 cm
Inscribed M. Hobbema 1659 · EU cat.717

If genuine the date of 1659 would make this painting a very early work, but x-rays show that it is painted over a still life which is held looks later than 1659. Colin Thompson (*Seeing is not Believing*, Edinburgh, 1981) argued that this meant the picture is a fake made up of units akin to Hobbema's later work. The presence of a painting under the present picture is however not in itself conclusive evidence that it is a fake. It has always been common practice for artists to reuse supports, whether panel or canvas, in time of need. It is also very difficult to judge the style and date of a painting simply from an x-ray, but this is the principal ground for the argument that this is a fake. Christopher Wright (Birmingham 1989) takes the opposite view and proposes that both this and the following picture, no.718, have been unfairly doubted and that the style and undoubted quality of this painting is consistent with Hobbema's early work. Listed as by Hobbema HdG no.150 and Christopher Wright (Birmingham 1989).

EXHIBITED: Edinburgh Institution 1819, lent James Erskine; *Seeing is not Believing*, Edinburgh 1981, NGS

A Wooded River Valley with two Fishermen

Oil on wood · 47 × 68.6 cm
inscribed M. Hobbema · EU cat.718
Sir James Erskine, 1823, lists 'Hobbema – Landscape with a large oak in the centre – water and distance to the right with a man fishing'.

Waagen (1854) considered the signature false, HdG agreed, but later reinstated the picture as 'genuine throughout'. Technical examination has cast doubt on the date of the picture. Christopher Wright (Birmingham 1989) argues however that although it is very like a picture in Nottingham, it is nevertheless sufficiently different from it to be an authentic version of the composition and not simply a later copy. Listed as by Hobbema Christopher Wright (Birmingham 1989)

EXHIBITED: Edinburgh Institution 1819

Meindert Hobbema *A Woody Lane, with a Thatched Cottage and a Pool*

Meindert Hobbema *A Wooded River Valley with two Fishermen*

After Giulio Romano
Battle Piece

After Giulio Romano

B. ROME 1492 — D. MANTUA 1546

Giulio was a pupil and assistant of Raphael and was instructed to complete works left unfinished by Raphael at the time of his death in 1520. Giulio established himself at Mantua, with Gonzaga patronage, in 1524, painting and supervising architectural and engineering projects including the Palazzo del Té.

Battle Piece

Oil on canvas · 47.5 × 63.5 cm · EU cat.714
Sir James Erskine, 1823, lists 'Large Battle Piece called Wouvermans' .

Probably an early copy of a group in the extensive fresco of the *Battle of Constantine and Maxentius* in the Vatican Stanze, which was completed by Giulio Romano after Raphael's death.

Jan van der Heyden

B. GORINCHEM 1637 — D. AMSTERDAM 1712

Van der Heyden travelled widely in the southern Netherlands and Germany, but he was mainly active in Amsterdam. His speciality was townscape and in it he combined architectural precision with rich painterly handling.

Wooded Park Landscape with Deer

Oil on wood · 22 × 28.7 cm
late 17th c. · EU cat.716

This is one of van der Heyden's rare paintings that is exclusively landscape. It is very similar in treatment to a landscape in the National Gallery, London. Christopher Wright states: 'There is at present no means of dating such pictures but they could be as late as the 1690s when fashions

Jan van der Heyden
Wooded Park Landscape with Deer

were changing and moving towards an ever increasing appreciation of careful technique for its own sake.' Listed as van der Heyden by HdeG no.297 and by Christopher Wright (Birmingham 1989)

EXHIBITED: *Dutch Landscape Painting*, Newcastle 1983, *Dutch Art in the Seventeenth Century: Images of a Golden Age in British Collections*, Birmingham 1989

Karel du Jardin

SEE PAGE 19

After du Jardin

A Farrier's Shop

Oil on canvas · 36.5 × 42 cm · EU cat.720
Sir James Erskine, 1823, lists 'Called C.D. Jardin – Entrance of a Village – a man showing an ox.'

A weak copy or imitation of du Jardin's work.

After du Jardin
A Farrier's Shop

Simon Willemsz Kick

B. DELFT 1603 — D. AMSTERDAM 1652

Kick worked mainly in Amsterdam. He was a little known painter related through marriage to Pieter Codde and William Duyster – the leading Amsterdam painters of soldiers' life. He is the author of a signed portrait of 1639 in the Rijskmuseum, and of several soldiering subjects in the manner of Jacob Duck.

Soldiers at Cards

Oil on wood · 44.5 × 61.6 cm · EU cat.721
This work was originally attributed to Johann le Duq (1600–1660) and was first given to Kick by Bredius and Bode (1889). Listed as by Kick by Christopher Wright (Birmingham 1989).

Simon Willemsz Kick
Soldiers at Cards

Pieter van der Leeuw

SEE PAGE 20

Jan Lievens

SEE PAGE 21

Johannes Lingelbach

B. FRANKFURT 1622 – D. 1674

Lingelbach was perhaps a pupil of Wouverman. He went to Amsterdam in 1637, Paris in 1642, Italy in 1644 and returned to Amsterdam in 1650. He was one of the younger Bamboccianti in Rome and specialised in painting figures and animals for other artists, such as the decorative landscapist Moucheron.

An Alehouse Door

Oil on canvas · 41.5 × 36 cm
signed 'I.B' · EU cat.724

The monogramme 'I.B.' on this picture could perhaps be 'L.B.' in which case the picture could be attributed to Leendert Brasser. There seems no reason to doubt the old attribution and the picture is listed as by Lingelbach by Christopher Wright (Birmingham 1989).

Adam Frans Van der Meulen

SEE PAGE 22

Johannes Lingelbach *An Alehouse Door*

Pieter Neefs

B. ANTWERP 1578 – D. ANTWERP 1656/61

Neefs was a pupil of Steenwick the Elder – painter of small architectural scenes on copper. He was elected member of the Antwerp Guild of Painters in 1610. Neefs's figures are often added by another hand. The figures in this painting are attributed to Van Thulden.

Interior of a Cathedral

Oil on Panel 29 × 39 cm · EU cat.726

Pieter Neefs
Interior of a Cathedral

Hendrick ten Oever

SEE PAGE 23

Gaspard Poussin (Gaspard Dughet)

SEE PAGE 24

Giulio Cesare Procaccini

SEE PAGE 25

Adam Pynacker

SEE PAGE 26

After Guido Reni

B. NEAR BOLOGNA 1575 – D. BOLOGNA 1642

Reni was one of the leading Bolognese painters in Rome during the first two decades of 17th c. and then the major easel painter in Bologna. Reni had a large studio which produced many versions of popular religious subjects, such as the Ecce Homo, and these were much copied.

Ecce Homo

Oil on canvas · 81.2 × 90 cm · EU cat.731

The National Gallery, London, has a version of this *Ecce Homo* which is of better quality.

After Guido Reni
Ecce Homo

Salvator Rosa

SEE PAGE 26

Jacob Isaacksz van Ruisdael

B. HAARLEM 1628/9 — D. HAARLEM 1682

Ruisdael was born in Haarlem and trained with his father Isaack and his uncle Salomon van Ruysdael. After travelling he settled in Amsterdam in 1655 and was both productive and very influential.

A Wood Scene

Oil on canvas · 61 × 74 cm
signed indistinctly 'Jv. Ruisdael 1649' · EU cat.733
This painting relates to works in Glasgow, Hamburg and Leningrad.

Banks of a River

ILLUSTRATED IN COLOUR ON PAGE 2

Oil on canvas · 134 × 193 cm
dated 1649 · EU cat.734

The basic composition is adapted from a painting of two years earlier, *River Landscape with a High Sandy Bank* (Hage Collection, Denmark). However, the dramatic high sky and extensive panorama give this picture a unique grandeur. Ruisdael used drawings of Rhenen on the Neder Rijn as the inspiration for the town in the distance, and the tower of the church of St. Cunera and twin towers of Rhenen's watergate are clearly visible. He also adapted various motifs from the work of Cornelis Vroom. The figures are probably painted by another artist, possibly Berchem, or Wouverman.

EXHIBITED: *Ruisdael*, 1981, NGS.; *Dutch Landscape – The Early Years*, 1986, National Gallery London; *Masters of Seventeenth Century Dutch Landscape Painting* 1987–88, Rijskmuseum, Boston & Philadelphia; *The Golden Age of Dutch Landscape Painting* 1995, Museo de Arte Thyssen-Bornemisza, Madrid.

After Hercules Seghers
Landscape

After Hercules Seghers

B. HAARLEM *c*.1590 — D. AMSTERDAM *c*.1640

Seghers studied with Conixloo in Amsterdam, entered the Haarlem Guild of St. Manticore Luke in 1612 and became one of the most imaginative and evocative etchers of landscape. His authentic paintings are extremely rare.

Landscape

Oil on wood · 28 × 39 cm · EU cat.737

Although the picture is related to Rembrandt's *Landscape with the Good Samaritan* and it is known that Rembrandt collected Segher's works, the Torrie picture may be a copy by Roelent Roghman (1620?–1692). It is listed as sketch for a *Mountain Landscape* in the 1909 catalogue and given as Rembrandt. It is also listed as Seghers by Christopher Wright (Birmingham 1989).

Frans Snyders

B. ANTWERP 1579 — D. ANTWERP 1657

After travelling in Italy 1608–9, Snyders worked for Rubens and for Jacob Jordaens and also produced many hunting scenes and still-life subjects of his own.

Wolf Hunt

Oil on canvas · 178 × 253 cm
EU cat.no. 735, pair to no.736

Frans Snyders
Wolf Hunt

The Boar Hunt

Oil on canvas · 178 × 253 cm
EU cat.736, pair to no.735

These paintings relate to a similar pair *A Wolf Hunt* and *A Boar Hunt* sold at Christie's 30 July 1976.

Unknown Artist, after Teniers, the Younger
A Pasticcio

Jan Steen
SEE PAGE 28

David Teniers the Younger
SEE PAGE 29

Unknown Artist, after Teniers the Younger

A Pasticcio

Oil on canvas · 29 × 44.5 cm · EU cat.740
A copy after Teniers. See no.739, p.29

Imitator of Francesco Vecellio

B. PIEVE DI CADORE *c*.1475 – D. VENICE
1559/60

Little known elder brother of Titian, he trained
with Giovanni Bellini. He also imitated
Giorgione and thereafter lived and worked very
much in the shadow of his famous sibling whose
work he imitated.

Virgin and Child with St Catherine

Oil on wood · 39 × 48 cm · EU cat.741
This picture has traditionally been attributed to
a follower of Titian. There is however no known
composition by Titian himself on which it could
be based. On the other hand it is closely related
to a painting attributed by Berenson and others
to Titian's elder brother, Francesco Vecellio, at
Hampton Court of the *Virgin and Child with St*

Imitator of Francesco Vecellio
Virgin and Child with St Catherine

Catherine and the infant John the Baptist. This was a
popular image as Wethey (*Paintings of Titian*, 3
vols., 1969, cat.x–20, p.174–5) lists no less than
seven variations of it. He does not include the
present picture however, although it repeats the
composition of the Hampton Court painting in
reverse, but without the figure of the infant
John the Baptist. The proportions of the
composition are changed slightly, reflecting this
omission. The background is also quite
different, as are the costume, hairstyles and
features of the figures. The composition does
otherwise reproduce faithfully the position of
the figures and the attitude of the heads
however. The only exception is in the position
of the Infant Christ's hands which have been
adapted to the gesture of taking flowers offered
to him which is the central gesture of Raphael's
Holy Family with a Palm Tree where the Infant
Christ is taking flowers from St Joseph who is
kneeling in an attitude very similar to that of St
Catherine here. The reversal of a composition
usually means that the picture is copied from an
engraving which is presumably the case here
though at the present time no engraving is
known.

Unknown Artist, Dutch School
Sea Piece

Oil on canvas · 40 × 56 cm
initialled A.V.V. · EU cat.711

The initials A.V.V., which have been read on the
picture in the past but now seem to be illegible,
suggest an attribution to Adrian van de Velde
(1636–72) who, though principally a painter of
small landscapes, was son and pupil of marine
painter William van de Velde the Elder, and is
known to have executed some beach scenes.
Waagen attributed the work to Jacob van
Ruisdael, HdG to Jean Porcellis. J.T. Blankerhof
has also been suggested.

Piero della Vecchia

B. VENICE 1606 – D. VENICE 1678

Pietro Muttoni known as Piero della Vecchia
was a pupil of Padovanini, but imitated
Giorgione.

The Lovers

Oil on canvas · 54.6 × 71 cm · EU cat.742

This picture was attributed to Giorgione by Sir
Jame Erskine. In 1823, he lists a 'Georgeona
representing two figures'. In the 1826 inventory

Piero della Vecchia
The Lovers

compiled by Andrew Wilson, this work again appears attributed to Giorgione and is described as 'Man and Woman'. In an 1848 inventory of pictures cleaned by O'Neill, it is also listed as by Giorgione 'A Noble and a Girl'.

Adrian van de Velde

B. 1636 AMSTERDAM — D. 1672

Van de Velde was the son of Willem van de Velde the Elder, the marine painter, and brother of Willem van de Velde the Younger. He was trained by his father and by Johannes Wynants and Paulus Potter, the animal painter. He probably did not go to Italy, but his work consists predominantly of pastoral landscape in the manner of the Dutch-Italianate painters.

Cattle and Herdsman

Oil on canvas · 30 × 37.5 cm · EU cat.743
Sir James Erskine, 1823, lists 'A Valdeveldt - Landscape with horses and cattle'. Listed by Wright as Adrian van der Velde (Birmingham 1989).

William van de Velde the younger

SEE PAGE 30

Studio of Paolo Veronese

SEE PAGE 31

Richard Wilson

SEE PAGE 32

Adrian van de Velde
Cattle and Herdsman

SCULPTURE

Francois Duquesnoy (il Flamingo)

B. BRUSSELS 1594 — D. EN ROUTE TO PARIS 1653

The leading non-Italian sculptor of the mid-17th c. in Italy, who worked in Rome from 1618 to 1643. A Baroque classicist and friend of Poussin, he was particularly famous for his putti.

Cupid

ILLUSTRATED IN COLOUR ON BACK COVER

Bronze h.37.1 cm · EU cat.644
The figure of Cupid has been detached from a version of the group of *Apollo and Cupid* executed by Duquesnoy as a pair to the better known *Mercury and Cupid* for Marchese Vincenzo Giustiniani. Only two versions of the *Apollo and Cupid* are known, one in the Lichtenstein Collection, the other in the Royal Palace, Madrid. Formerly covered with green paint to simulate corrosion and give a fake-antique patina, the *Cupid* seems to have been sold to Sir James Erskine in Rome around 1800 as a classical bronze. Its authenticity as by the hand of Duquesnoy is, however, substantiated by a mention in Bellori's biography of the sculptor. It is clear that the Cupids and accessories were always cast separately and fixed onto the main figure which rendered them prone to removal later. Several other detached Cupids by Duquesnoy exist.

EXHIBITED: *Effigies and Ecstasies: Roman Baroque Sculpture and Design in the Age of Bernini*, 1998, NGS.

Circle of Giovanni da Bologna (Jean de Boulogne) known as Giambologna

SEE PAGE 14

Unknown Sculptor after Giambologna

Mercury

Bronze h.57.2 cm · EU cat.646
Originally thought to be a reduced copy of the large bronze by Giambologna in Florence of which many copies from all periods exist, this bronze is in fact derived from a small bronze *Mercury* made by Giambologna for Emperor Maximilian II in 1565, now in the Kunsthistorisches Museum in Vienna. The Torrie bronze appears to be an excellent and rare

Florentine cast of the 17th c., produced by one of Giambologna's successors in his workshop. The bronze is slightly smaller than the three documented autograph versions of this model in Vienna, Naples and Dresden.

Francois Marie Ponçet

B. LYONS 1736 — D. MARSEILLE 1797

Ponçet studied in Marseille and then in Paris, but though he twice failed to win the Prix de Rome, eventually went to Rome independently in 1760. He was elected to the Academy degli Arcadi in Rome in 1771. In 1775 he returned to Paris, becoming a member of the Lyons Academy on the way. In 1777 he returned to Rome, but was also elected to the Bologna Academy. He left Italy in 1789, returning first to Paris and then Marseille.

Venus after the Bath 1771

Marble h.0.718 m, inscribed underneath the base F.M. PONCET A ROME 1771 · EU cat.665
This work predates other recorded works by Ponçet by 5 years. Strongly classical in inspiration, it is an important and very early piece of French neo-classicism reflecting the fact that it was made in Rome where Ponçet was clearly in touch with artists in the circle of Gavin Hamilton such as the sculptor Tobias Serghells. He was no doubt also influenced by the ideas of

Unknown Sculptor after Giambologna
Mercury

Massimiliano Soldani
Arrotino

Massimiliano Soldani
Virtue Triumphant over Vice

Winckelmann. Another marble *Venus* by Ponçet, dated 1778, is in the Musée Cognacq-Jay, Paris. The contents of Ponçet's studio in Paris were sold in 1800. This is likely to have been the source from which the work came. Sir James most probably acquired it from an intermediary when he was in Paris with the Duke of Wellington in 1815.

Massimiliano Soldani

B. FLORENCE 1658 — D. FLORENCE 1740

Soldani trained in the studio of Ercole Ferrata (1610–86) and produced many small bronzes in his Florentine workshop; he was particularly noted for his small bronze reductions from classical marbles.

The Wrestlers

Bronze h.41 cm · EU cat.647, pair to no.648
The Wrestlers is a reduced version of the antique marble in the Uffizi. A characteristic and high quality work.

Arrotino

Bronze h.36.8 cm · EU cat.648, pair to no.647
This is a reduced version of the antique marble *Arrotino* in the Uffizi. An alternative attribution to the Susini workshop is given by Sotheby's (1992).

Virtue Triumphant over Vice

Bronze h.30.6 cm.
EU cat.649
This work is a fine bronze reduction with variations by Soldani of the marble group of 1570 *Florence Triumphant over Pisa*, popularly known as *Virtue and Vice*, by Giambologna, in the Bargello, Florence. Another slightly smaller version of the same group by Soldani is in the Frick Collection, New York. It is common for bases of Soldani bronzes to differ slightly, however, (Radcliffe) and in all other respects the two casts are identical.

Attributed to Antonio Susini

D. 1624

Susini was foreman to Giambologna, and with his nephew Gianfrancesco Susini (d. 1646), made many small bronze versions of classical statues of this type.

Boar

Bronze h.15.8 cm · EU cat.655
A reduction from the antique marble boar in the Uffizi known as the Florentine Boar. Considered by Anthony Radcliffe to be a product of the Susini workshop. A signed version in the V&A, and a version of 'superb quality' at Castle Howard are connected to the poorer quality Torrie bronze.

Massimiliano Soldani
The Wrestlers

Attributed to Antonio Susini
Boar

Susini workshop after Michelangelo

Dawn

Bronze h.28 cm, l.73.5 cm
EU cat.660, pair to no.661

Night

Bronze l. 60 cm · EU cat.661 pair to no.660
These are reduced versions of Michelangelo's *Dawn* and *Night* in the Medici Chapel, San Lorenzo, Florence. Many small bronze versions of these sculptures from all periods exist. These are however good copies, and although previously catalogued as by an unknown sculptor, were convincingly reattributed by Sotheby's (1992 valuation) to the workshop of Susini, c1600.

Adrian de Vries

SEE PAGE 16

Unknown Sculptor

He Goat

Bronze h.18 cm · EU cat.653
Not as originally listed in 1909 catalogue, an antique, nor, as was later thought, a 16th c. bronze, but an Italian fake of the 18th c. clearly from the same foundry as the *Bull*, no.654.

Unknown Sculptor

Bull

Bronze h.25.7 cm · EU cat.654
An Italian fake of the 18th c. clearly from the same foundry as the *Goat*, no.653. Cast after the well known bronze bull by Giambologna, with deliberate flaws introduced and with a chemically induced fake antique patina. Fake antiques of this type were very popular with collectors and provide a fascinating insight into 18th c. taste.

Unknown Sculptor

A Roman Empress

Bronze head set in marble bust
h.82.5 cm · EU cat.656
This superb bronze has yet to be investigated. Originally identified as Empress Plotina, Consort of Trajan, it is now thought that the head is a Roman Baroque work, though the marble bust may be antique.

Unknown Sculptor

Rape of a Sabine

Bronze h.59.5 cm · EU cat.657
A 17th c. version of the small bronze of the same subject by Giambologna. Most likely an Italian cast, but conceivably French and from the same foundry as *Astronomy*, no.658

Unknown Sculptor
He Goat

Unknown Sculptor

Astronomy

Bronze h.37.5 cm · EU cat.658
A late version of Giambologna's small bronze, *Astronomy*, and from the same foundry as the *Rape of a Sabine*, no.657. A finer version in Vienna is larger – 38.8 cm. The French origin is suggested by the dark red patina.

Unknown Sculptor

Alcibiades, The Fighting Gladiator

Bronze h.73.5 cm · EU cat.659
A reduced version of the Borghese Warrior now in the Louvre, which, when it was in the Villa Borghese (until 1806) was known as the *Gladiatore*. This cast is probably Italian, but might also possibly be French.

Unknown Sculptor

Venus de Medici

Bronze h.61 cm · EU cat.662
A bronze reduced copy after the antique marble *Venus de Medici* in the Uffizi. This was one of the few surviving antique marbles in Florence and a prime attraction for Grand Tourists of the 18th c. This work was very likely made for that market.

Unknown Sculptor
Venus de Medici

Unknown Sculptor

Punishment of Dirce

Bronze h.21 cm · EU cat.663
A late eighteenth century reduction of the classical marble known as the *Farnese Bull* now in the Naples Museum. This type of well made bronze was very popular as country house furnishing, to complement decor and pictures, and to reflect the owner's educated taste for classical art.

Unknown Sculptor
Alcibiades, The Fighting Gladiator

Unknown Sculptor, after Michelangelo

Slave

Bronze h.20.4 cm · EU cat.664
Small bronze copy of one of Michelangelo's Slaves for the tomb of Pope Julius II. A poor quality bronze of around 1800(?) listed in the 1909 catalogue as 'Miniature of a Youth with one arm on his head and the other behind his head'.

Unknown Sculptor

Antique draped Female, without head or arms

Parian Marble h.80.5 cm · EU cat.666

Unknown Sculptor

Torso of a Venus

Black Marble h.86 cm · EU cat.667
Probably antique and listed as 'Antique marble of a nude Venus' in 1909 catalogue.

Unknown Sculptor

Statue of a Youth

Marble h.50.5 cm,
EU cat.668
Listed as 'Antique small statue of a youth' in 1909 catalogue, but possibly a Bacchus of 2nd c. AD

Unknown Sculptor

Draped Figure

Marble h.53 cm · EU cat.669
Listed as ' Antique small draped Figure' in 1909 catalogue.

Unknown Sculptor

Draped Venus

Marble h.28 cm · EU cat.670
Listed as 'Small antique figure of a Draped Venus' in 1909 catalogue.

Unknown Sculptor

Arria and Paetus

Italian Marble h.96.5 cm · EU cat.671
Listed as 'Group of Arria and Paetus, in Italian Marble' in 1909 catalogue.

Unknown Sculptor

Crouching Venus

Carrara Marble h.43.5 cm · EU cat.672
Listed as 'Copy of the Crouching Venus, in Carrara marble' in 1909 catalogue.

VASES

Giacomo Zoffoli
Three vases

Unknown Sculptor

Vase

Verde Antico Porphyry h.66 cm · EU cat.675

Unknown Sculptor

Small Vase

Verde Antico Porphyry h.33 cm · EU cat.676

Unknown Sculptor

Small Vase

Verde Antico Porphyry h.33 cm · EU cat.677

Unknown Sculptor

Vase

Grey Granite h.40.4 cm · EU cat.678, pair to no.679

Unknown Sculptor

Vase

Grey Granite h.40.4 cm · EU cat.679, pair to no.678

Unknown Sculptor

Vase

Rosso Antico Marble h.50.25 cm · EU cat.680

Unknown Sculptor

Vase with Handles

Rosso Antico Porphyry h.48.5 cm d. at mouth 30.5cm · EU cat.681, pair to no.682

Unknown Sculptor

Vase with Handles

Rosso Antico Porphyry h.48.4 cm d. at mouth 30.5cm · EU cat.682, pair to no.681

Giacomo Zoffoli

B. *c.*1731 – D. ROME 1784

Giacomo worked in partnership with Giovanni Zoffoli (b. 1745–d.Rome 1805) who was his brother or perhaps uncle. The two Zoffolis produced in their studio in Rome many bronze statuettes and vases based on antique marbles for the benefit of tourists and collectors.

Vase

Bronze h.34.5 cm, inscribed G. ZOFFOLI F. EU cat.650

This is a rare and high quality bronze reduced copy of the *Medici Vase* (formerly in Villa Medici, Rome, now in Uffizi). In the Zoffoli list of models of 1795, this design figures as no.41. Another example forms part of a garniture de cheminée in the Saloon at Saltram Park, Devon and was bought in Rome by Lord Boringdon in 1793.

Vase

Bronze h.32.6 cm, inscribed G ZOFFOLI F. EU cat.651

The design is adapted from the *Gaeta Vase*, now in the Naples Museum. The model (which adds handles) figures as no.45 in the list of models offered for sale by the Zoffoli foundry in 1795, preserved by the V&A Museum, but it is very rare – no other example is known. It clearly forms a set with Nos. 650 and and 652 to be exhibited as a garniture de cheminée.

Vase

Bronze 34.2 cm · EU cat.652

This is a reduced copy of the *Borghese Vase*, formerly in the Villa Borghese, Rome, and since 1806 in the Louvre. The design figures as no.42 in the Zoffoli list of models of 1795, but is rare.

MISCELLANEOUS ITEMS

Unknown Sculptor

Pedestal

Verde Antico Porphyry h.34.5 cm · EU cat.673

Not in 1909 catalogue as a separate unit, but listed by NGS as part of the Torrie Collection as 'Pedestal in Verde Antico Porphyry'.

Unknown Sculptor

Base with Small Fluted Column

Marble h.19.5 cm · EU cat.674

Fluted column surmounting small stepped base broken off at around 5 inches. Labels give the base a Torrie provenance. There is a small hole through the centre of the column, probably for the attachment of a statuette.